U.S. NAVAL SPECIAL WARFARE FORCES

SANDY DONOVAN

LERNER PUBLICATIONS COMPANY / MINNEAPOLIS

CHAPTER OPENER PHOTO CAPTIONS

Cover: A SEAL ascends to the surface from the USS *Kamehameha,* a nuclear-powered submarine.

Ch. 1: U.S. Navy F9F Panther jet fighters prepare to land aboard the USS *Boxer* aircraft carrier after returning from a mission during the Korean War (1950–1953).

Ch. 2: All U.S. Navy recruits must take an oath to defend the United States.

Ch. 3: Physical fitness is a vital part of U.S. Naval Special Warfare forces training.

Ch. 4: Navy SEALs land on a riverbank during a training operation.

Acknowledgments
Thanks to NCC (SW) Bryan Niepoetter for his help in preparing this book.

Copyright © 2005 by Sandy Donovan

Lerner Publications Company
A division of Lerner Publishing Group
241 First Avenue North
Minneapolis, MN 55401

Website address: www.lernerbooks.com

Library of Congress Cataloging-in-Publication Data

Donovan, Sandra, 1967–
    U.S. Naval Special Warfare Forces / by Sandy Donovan
      p.   cm. — (U.S. Armed Forces)
    Includes biographical references and index.
    Contents: History—Recruitment—Training—Life in the Naval Special Warfare Forces.
    ISBN: 0-8225-1650-0 (lib. bdg. : alk. paper)
    1. Special forces (Military science)—United States—Juvenile literature. 2. United States. Navy—Commando troops—Juvenile literature. [1. Special forces (Military science) 2. United States. Navy—Commando troops.] I. Title. II. U.S. Armed Forces (Series : Lerner Publications)
    VG87.D66 2005
    359.9'84'0973—dc22   2003019642

Manufactured in the United States of America
1 2 3 4 5 6 – JR – 10 09 08 07 06 05

CONTENTS

chapter ONE
HISTORY

A **NAVY SPECIALIZES** in fighting on or near the water. All navies have fleets of ships and boats. Some also have fleets of aircraft.

Like the U.S. Army and the U.S. Air Force, the U.S. Navy has a group of special teams that take on special missions (jobs). These missions include making secret attacks, rescuing prisoners from the enemy, and capturing important enemy leaders. The navy calls its teams Special Warfare forces. Naval Special Warfare forces are some of the toughest, best-trained, and most-skilled soldiers and sailors in the world.

THE BIRTH OF THE U.S. NAVY

The U.S. Navy is more than 200 years old. The country's first navy, known as the Continental Navy, was formed in 1775. It was created to fight the British during the American Revolution (1775–1783). In 1794 the U.S. government officially created the U.S. Navy.

Throughout the 1800s, the navy was one of the most important branches of the U.S. armed forces. By the 1900s, the United States had one of the world's largest and most powerful navies.

The Continental Navy's *Bonhomme Richard (right)* defeats the British *Serapis (left)* in 1779 during the American Revolution.

The Japanese surprise attack on the U.S. naval base at Pearl Harbor in December 1941 brought the United States into World War II.

WORLD WAR II: THE BEGINNING OF THE NAVAL SPECIAL WARFARE FORCES

World War II (1939–1945) was the largest and most violent war in history. Armies, navies, and air forces fought on land, at sea, and in the air in Europe, Asia, northern Africa, and the Atlantic and Pacific Oceans. The Allies—the United States, Great Britain, the Soviet Union, and others—fought the Axis powers—Germany, Japan, Italy, and others. Such a widespread war needed many highly trained soldiers who could perform special missions. The navy began to train some of its toughest, strongest, and smartest men for these missions. (Women were not allowed to serve on ships in combat zones during this time.) The navy split the men into small units. These units would later come to be known as Naval Special Warfare forces, or special forces. Their missions were called special operations, or special ops. Members of the special forces were called special operatives.

During the war, the navy's special forces performed many different kinds of missions. Most of these were amphibious operations. They took place on land, at sea, and sometimes in the air. Many of the war's biggest battles began with amphibious landings. Huge Allied armies, riding in boats called landing craft, stormed enemy beaches in North Africa, Europe, and on islands in the Pacific Ocean.

Navy special forces teams played a key role in these landings. U.S. Navy Scout and Raider units hit the beaches before an invasion. Working under cover of darkness, they mapped out the beaches. They found the best places to land troops. They put up markers to show the landing craft where to land.

Scout units such as the one above helped special forces during World War II by gathering information about landing spots.

The enemy often placed obstacles on the beach to slow down landing craft. So Scout and Raider units did demolition work. They blew up the obstacles. Sometimes the enemy set mines—explosive devices—in the water. Scout and Raider units had to disarm (shut down) these mines to keep them from destroying the landing craft.

U.S. Navy combat demolition units (NCDUs) had a similar job. NCDUs had to clear the beaches of German-controlled Normandy, France, for the Allied D-Day invasion of June 6, 1944. The best landing areas were heavily defended by German troops. On one of the landing beaches, German troops killed or wounded more than half the NCDU forces. But the teams got the job done, and the invasion was a success. Less than a year after the invasion, Allied troops had pushed through Europe and defeated Germany.

U.S. forces prepare to land on one of four beaches in Normandy, France, on D-Day 1944.

UDT and NCDU operatives had a number of nicknames. Sometimes they were called naked warriors because they wore only swimsuits and goggles. They were also called frogmen because their swim fins made them look like frogs.

Underwater demolition teams (UDTs) did a similar job in the Pacific. They often worked underwater and wore swimsuits, swim fins, and goggles. Like other units, they mapped and cleared beaches. UDTs also infiltrated (passed through) enemy waters and enemy territory to destroy important Japanese targets.

World War II also saw the beginning of what later came to be known as special boat units (SBUs). The navy began to use smaller, faster boats in World War II. Called patrol torpedo (PT) boats, these vessels performed many different kinds of missions. Using their torpedoes—missiles that traveled underwater—PT boats could strike and sink larger enemy ships. PT boats also picked up and dropped off Scout and Raider units and UDTs on infiltration missions.

By the summer of 1945, Allied forces had pushed the Japanese out of most of its bases in Asia and the Pacific Ocean. The conflict continued until September of that year. Japan surrendered, officially ending World War II.

U.S. forces invaded Inchon near dawn on September 15, 1950. They quickly seized the port from the North Koreans.

KOREAN AND VIETNAM WARS: BIRTH OF THE SEALS

During the Korean War (1950–1953), U.S. forces were called on to defend South Korea from an invasion by North Korea. UDTs and PT boats played an important role in the amphibious landing at Inchon, the turning point of the war. The navy's special operations teams also performed infiltration and demolition missions.

In the 1960s, the United States began sending troops to Vietnam to fight in the Vietnam War (1954–1975). This war was fought between North Vietnam and its supporters and South Vietnam and its supporters. The United States fought alongside South Vietnam. Much of the fighting involved guerrilla warfare. Small groups of fighters, called guerrillas, struck fast before disappearing into the Vietnamese jungle. To fight this war, the United States needed highly trained special forces units.

In 1962 U.S. president John F. Kennedy ordered all of the armed forces to train units in unconventional, or guerrilla, warfare. Some of the UDTs kept

President John F. Kennedy oversaw the expansion of U.S. special forces units in the early 1960s.

doing their usual tasks. Others were given additional training to fight guerrilla wars. These new units were named SEALs, which stands for Sea, Air, and Land. SEALs are trained to move through water, through the air, and on land. They can parachute out of airplanes or rappel (slide down ropes) out of helicopters. They can also swim underwater using scuba (self-contained underwater breathing apparatus) gear or move on land, on foot, or in vehicles.

SEALs are the best-trained soldiers in the U.S. Navy. They specialize in

ADVISERS

Special forces do more than just fight. They also train other soldiers in unconventional warfare. During the Vietnam War, SEALs and UDTs spent much of their time as advisers. They advised, or taught, both U.S. and Vietnamese troops how to parachute, swim, fight, plant explosives, and perform other skills.

During peacetime, SEALs and other special forces teams spend most of their time training and advising other soldiers. They are constantly working on new ways to fight and pass on their knowledge to others.

reconnaissance (observation or spying) missions and guerrilla attacks on enemy forces. In Vietnam, patrol boats inserted (dropped off) SEAL teams at certain points, usually along one of Vietnam's many rivers. From there the SEALs infiltrated enemy territory and staged attacks. They also rescued shot-down pilots or mapped out the area for a larger attack. SEAL teams often blew up enemy equipment, bases, and communication lines before disappearing back into the jungle.

To help with SEAL missions, the navy developed more special boat units. One kind of unit sailed special boats called patrol boats, riverine (PBR). PBRs were built to travel on Vietnam's narrow, shallow rivers. Another kind of boat unit was the SEAL delivery vehicle (SDV) team. SEAL delivery vehicles were small submarines, made for infiltrating enemy territory underwater.

Two SEALs pause for a drink of water while performing their duties in the Vietnam War.

A U.S. Navy armored boat patrols the waters of the Saigon River during the Vietnam War.

At the time, these boat units were often called the Brown Water Navy because the rivers they worked in were brown and muddy. U.S. forces left Vietnam in 1973. North Vietnam eventually defeated South Vietnam in 1975.

THE 1980S TO THE 1990S: NAVY SPECIAL FORCES AROUND THE WORLD

In 1983 the U.S. government sent U.S. Naval Special Warfare forces to the Caribbean island of Grenada. A group of rebels (antigovernment forces) had staged a coup, or overthrow, of the government. They killed Grenada's leader and took over the country. Grenada's neighbors—the island nations of Jamaica, Barbados, Barbuda, Antigua, Saint Lucia, Dominica, and Saint Vincent and the Grenadines—were concerned that the new Grenadian government was a threat to them. Also, many U.S. citizens lived on the island and attended a medical school there. The United States was afraid these U.S. medical students might be taken hostage by the new Grenadian government. So the United States and Grenada's neighbors sent in troops to rescue the students and to remove the new government.

SEAL units helped lead the invasion. They scouted a beach for the main invasion force. They also knocked out a radio station to keep the enemy from communicating during the attack. The invasion was successful, and the mission ended after only three days.

Six years later, in 1989, Naval Special Warfare forces took on another tough operation. U.S. forces invaded Panama to capture the country's leader, General Manuel Noriega. The United States accused Noriega of running a huge drug-smuggling operation across U.S. borders.

In Panama the SEALs had to keep Noriega from escaping. One SEAL team destroyed the general's two

OPERATIONS

Big military missions are called operations. Every operation is given a special code name. Here are some code names of important operations in history:

D-Day invasion = Operation Overlord (1944)

Inchon landing = Operation Chromite (1950)

Grenada = Operation Urgent Fury (1983)

Panama = Operation Just Cause (1989)

Persian Gulf War = Operation Desert Storm (1991)

Somalia = Operation Restore Hope (1992–1994)

Afghanistan = Operation Enduring Freedom (2001)

Iraq = Operation Iraqi Freedom (2003)

fast boats. Another unit was supposed to destroy Noriega's jet airplane. But this team ran into trouble. They were attacked as they approached the airport. Panamanian forces killed four SEALs, and the mission failed. But other U.S. forces caught Noriega before he could escape. The general was brought to the United States. He was tried, convicted, and sent to prison for his crimes.

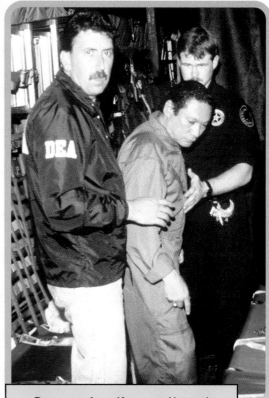

Panamanian dictator Manuel Noriega was arrested by the Drug Enforcement Administration.

Two years later, Naval Special Warfare forces were called into action in the Middle East. In 1990 Iraqi forces had invaded Iraq's neighbor, Kuwait. The United States formed a coalition (group) of countries to push Iraqi forces out of Kuwait. U.S. president George H. W. Bush ordered Iraqi president Saddam Hussein to remove his troops from Kuwait. Saddam refused, so the coalition attacked on January 17, 1991. The conflict was called the Persian Gulf War.

Once again, Naval Special Warfare forces played a key role. Their most important mission was to create a diversion, or a distraction. Coalition forces wanted the Iraqis to think they were making an amphibious attack

A U.S. Navy diver attaches an explosive to the side of an Iraqi mine in the Persian Gulf during Operation Desert Storm. Navy divers destroyed hundreds of Iraqi mines during the 1991 war.

on a Kuwaiti beach. So SEALs crept onto the beach and planted explosives. When the explosives went off, Iraqi leaders thought the coalition was making its landing. The Iraqis sent troops to attack, but the landing never occurred. Instead, coalition forces hit a different area. The diversion had caused the Iraqis to spread their defenses, making it easier for the coalition to smash through them. The coalition drove Iraqi forces out of Kuwait in six weeks.

In the early 1990s, Naval Special Warfare forces went into action in the East African nation of Somalia. Somalia was locked in a brutal civil (internal) war. Millions of Somalis were left homeless and starving. Organizations such as the International Red Cross and the United Nations (UN) wanted to bring food and medicine to Somalia. But the civil war made this work too dangerous. So U.S. forces, including SEAL teams, went to help the humanitarian mission. They protected UN and Red Cross workers while they delivered aid.

FIGHTING TERRORISM

On September 11, 2001, terrorists attacked the United States at the World Trade Center towers in New York and the Pentagon near Washington, D.C. The U.S. government believes that a group called al-Qaeda was responsible for the attacks. In 2001 al-Qaeda ran a number of bases in the central Asian country of Afghanistan. There they trained men to be terrorists. The Taliban, the Afghan government, supported al-Qaeda.

After the September 11 attacks, U.S. president George W. Bush demanded that the Taliban destroy the al-Qaeda bases and hand over al-Qaeda members living in Afghanistan. The Taliban refused. So in October 2001, U.S. troops invaded the country.

A SEAL provides cover for his teammates while attacking Taliban forces in Afghanistan in early 2002.

SEAL teams spent much of the war on "search and destroy" missions. When U.S. forces spotted al-Qaeda or Taliban fighters, they sent in the SEALs. Helicopters inserted the SEALs, who then hunted down the enemy. SEAL teams killed and captured many terrorists. They also found many caves and hideouts where al-Qaeda and Taliban fighters had hidden weapons and explosives. U.S. forces drove the Taliban out of power and destroyed al-Qaeda's terrorist bases. After the war, a new government was created in Afghanistan.

In 2003 U.S. leaders were still concerned about Saddam Hussein. They believed the Iraqi president had weapons of mass destruction (WMD)—weapons that could be used in a terrorist attack to kill thousands or even millions of people.

SEALs discover a large supply of munitions in a cave during a search-and-destroy mission in Afghanistan in 2002.

After the Persian Gulf War in 1991, Saddam had agreed to destroy his WMD and not make any more such weapons. But Saddam's government did not cooperate with weapons inspectors. Once again, the U.S. formed a coalition to destroy Saddam's government and to help the Iraqi people create a new government. In March 2003, coalition forces invaded the country.

Naval Special Warfare forces search an Iraqi ship for weapons at the port of Umm Qasr in Iraq in 2003.

Naval Special Warfare forces were given the job of capturing the Iraqi seaport of Umm Qasr. SEALs and SBUs infiltrated the port, taking prisoners and capturing weapons. Within a few days, they had taken control of Umm Qasr. This allowed the coalition to send in ships to deliver food and medicine to the Iraqi people.

By April 2003, Saddam Hussein's government had been destroyed. U.S. forces captured him in December. Meanwhile, anticoalition guerrillas continued to attack coalition troops and the Iraqis who were helping them. In 2004 SEAL teams are taking on search-and-destroy missions to find and destroy these fighters.

chapter TWO

RECRUITMENT

NOT EVERYONE CAN JOIN the U.S.
Naval Special Warfare forces. To qualify, members must
be smart, courageous, and physically fit. They must be
able to pass demanding physical and mental tests and
have the smarts to learn many different skills. Most
important, they must be able to work in high-stress
situations.

Only the best recruits (new members) become part
of the U.S. Naval Special Warfare forces. But the first
step to joining one of these teams is to join the U.S.

Navy. Once they become members of the navy, recruits go through special training to be considered for the SEALs, SBUs, or other units.

Joining the armed forces is a big decision. So candidates usually talk to a school counselor or a navy recruiter to see if enlisting is the right choice for them. Most high school counselors can provide candidates with information on U.S. Navy careers and U.S. Navy life. Most cities also have U.S. Navy Recruiting Centers, where candidates can learn more about serving in the U.S. Navy. Counselors and recruiters can also explain the special requirements for joining the U.S. Naval Special Warfare forces.

High school students can learn about the U.S. Navy at college fairs. Events are held on college campuses throughout the country.

THE NAVAL RESERVE VS. ACTIVE DUTY

A person can join the U.S. Navy as either a full-time member or as a member of the U.S. Naval Reserve.

Naval Reserve recruits attend a class on military rank structure. The program teaches new reservists about the navy.

About 380,000 people serve full-time in the navy, making up the bulk of the navy's force. Most of them live on navy bases or on navy ships. For these people, the navy is their full-time job. Some spend their entire careers in the navy.

About 150,000 people serve in the U.S. Naval Reserve. Reservists earn extra money while working part-time for the navy. Reservists live at home and have regular jobs. But they train with the navy for one weekend a month and two weeks each year. In times of war or disaster, reservists may be called up to full-time active duty.

Most special forces operatives serve in the navy full-time. But the U.S. Naval Special Warfare forces do have a small force of reservists. Most navy special forces reservists are former full-timers, who still want to serve their country part-time.

JOINING THE NAVY AS AN ENLISTEE

An enlistee is a person who enlists in (joins) the navy as a sailor instead of as an officer. About 95 percent of all navy recruits join as enlistees. A candidate must be a high school graduate between the ages of 17 and 34 (17-year-olds need parental permission). To qualify for the SEALs, a candidate must be a U.S. citizen. The U.S. government allows only men to serve in the SEALs or special boat units. Women are not allowed in frontline combat units.

At the beginning of basic training, each new enlistee receives navy gear such as boots and uniforms.

But women can still serve in the navy on ships in combat zones. And women can still be a part of the U.S. Naval Special Warfare forces. Many women serve in the special forces in noncombat, support roles. Women serve in the special forces as mechanics, equipment operators, and in other important jobs.

Everyone who wants to join the armed forces takes an exam called the Armed Services Vocational Aptitude Battery (ASVAB) Test. The ASVAB tests math, reading, mechanical ability, and other important skills. It also tests a person's aptitude, or intelligence. The U.S. Navy uses each recruit's ASVAB scores to match the recruit to jobs that will best fit their skills.

Recruits who want to join the special forces must show that they are

WOMEN IN THE NAVY SPECIAL FORCES

By law, women cannot be members of frontline combat units. So they cannot join special forces combat teams such as the SEALs and SBUs. But women who are interested in an exciting and unusual navy job *(above)* may attend the Naval School Explosive Ordnance Disposal (EOD). The school teaches men and women how to detect, identify, and disarm all kinds of weapons, including underwater explosives, chemical weapons, biological weapons, and nuclear weapons. Like SEALS, EOD candidates go through tough training and testing before they begin their service.

physically fit by passing a physical screening test (PST). This tough test requires recruits to swim, perform push-ups, sit-ups, and pull-ups, and run a long distance—all in a short period of time.

Next, every candidate has to choose what special job skills to learn. Jobs in the navy are called ratings. The navy has about 60 ratings. These include high-tech jobs such as electronics or computers. They can also involve a skill such as intelligence (spying) or weaponry.

Special forces candidates have to choose from a group of about 20 ratings, called source ratings. Source ratings are the kind of jobs needed for Naval Special Warfare forces teams. They include boatswain's mate, who is responsible for general maintenance of a ship's deck and external structures. It includes the electrician's mate, who repairs and operates a ship's electrical power plant and electrical equipment. Other

Boatswain's mates are responsible for general ship maintenance, such as tightening chain stops attached to anchor chains *(above)*.

An aviation antisubmarine warfare operator studies
an aviation flight manual during a mission.

SEAL source ratings are very specialized, such as
aviation antisubmarine warfare operator. Men who hold
this job operate airborne radar and electronic equipment
to locate and track submarines.

After the recruit joins the U.S. Navy, the recruit must
still pass many tests before becoming a member of the
special forces. To keep track of their goals, special forces
candidates receive a document called a challenge contract.
The challenge contract explains exactly what the recruit
must do to become a member of the special forces.

JOINING THE NAVY AS AN OFFICER

Another way to join the navy is to join as an officer.
Officers are the navy's leaders. A recruit who has
graduated from college can enter the navy as either a
regular officer or a reserve officer.

To become an officer, a candidate must be at least 19
years old and no older than 35 years old. He or she

must be a U.S. citizen. All U.S. Navy officers are college graduates. Most candidates study to become an officer while still in college. Others train as officers after graduating. The U.S. Navy has programs for both of these options. Whatever training program a candidate chooses, the person must get excellent grades in college. The navy only accepts good students into its officer program.

The Naval Reserve Officer Training Corps (ROTC) allows candidates to train as officers while they are in college. ROTC units are located at colleges and universities across the country. This four-year program also helps students pay for their schooling. ROTC students take civilian (nonmilitary) college courses. They also take military classes, such as military history, combat tactics, and leadership training.

Naval ROTC programs are available at more than 100 colleges throughout the United States.

UNIFORMS

ALL ON-DUTY NAVAL PERSONNEL are expected to be in uniform. A member's name, rank, and job can all be learned by a quick glance at the typical navy uniform. But navy special forces members often wear special clothing and gear while on a mission.

BATTLE DRESS UNIFORM

Most special forces personnel wear battle dress uniforms (BDUs). BDUs are made of tough material and have many pockets for carrying equipment and ammunition. The uniform's color and design—called camouflage—help the wearer to blend in with surroundings. Special forces personnel need this kind of camouflage to move around in enemy territory without being seen.

VESTS

Many SEALs wear vests for carrying extra equipment. This assault vest has many different pouches for carrying grenades (small explosive devices), demolition devices, ammunition, radios, and survival gear. SEALs often wear a tactical flotation vest. These vests can be used to keep a SEAL afloat when he has to swim long distances.

WET SUIT

When SEALs have to work underwater, they often wear wet suits made of neoprene, a kind of rubber. The suits not only keep SEALs dry, they also keep them warm. The ocean is very cold. Swimming without proper clothing can lead to deadly hypothermia (low body temperature). Wet suits are often worn with scuba gear, a mask, and flippers.

Students apply for the ROTC program when they apply for college. To be accepted, a candidate has to earn good grades in high school and score above average on either the SAT or ACT. The candidate needs referral letters from school counselors and needs to ace an officer interview. He or she must also pass a physical exam. When naval ROTC recruits graduate, they are given an officer's commission (a document granting them military rank and authority) in the U.S. Navy.

Another way to become a navy officer is to study at the U.S. Naval Academy in Annapolis, Maryland. The academy is one of the country's top schools. Only the best candidates earn a spot there. To become a midshipman (student at the academy), a candidate has to earn excellent grades and score well on college entrance exams, such as the Scholastic Aptitude Test. The candidate must also receive a recommendation from

Officer candidates at the U.S. Naval Academy read a guide for midshipmen while waiting to receive their uniforms.

a congressperson from his or her home state. U.S. Naval Academy graduates receive officer commissions in the navy.

A third way to become a naval officer is through Officer Candidate School (OCS). This is a challenging 13-week course for college graduates. The OCS program mixes classroom work and physical training. Officer Candidate School graduates receive commissions in the U.S. Navy. Most

Candidates must pass difficult tests before they can become officers in the U.S. Naval Special Warfare forces.

navy officers serve about six years. Some may spend their entire careers in the navy.

Becoming an officer is just the first step toward joining the special forces. Like enlistees, officers must learn valuable skills and pass tough tests in order to become members of the U.S. Naval Special Warfare forces. Only the best will make the cut.

chapter THREE

TRAINING

NAVY LIFE BEGINS with boot camp at the U.S. Navy's Recruit Training Command in Great Lakes, Illinois. For the next eight weeks, recruits will learn the ins and outs of life in the navy.

Boot camp is focused on discipline, both mental and physical. Discipline is important in combat situations. Mental discipline means staying cool under pressure. Physical discipline involves pushing your body to its limits.

Recruits also learn about the importance of teamwork.

To defeat the enemy, sailors and officers need to work as a team in combat.

BOOT CAMP

The first few days of boot camp are called in-processing. During in-processing, recruits officially become part of the navy. They take physical exams and receive haircuts and a navy sweat suit. All recruits wear sweat suits until they are given a uniform.

During boot camp, recruits live together in large housing units called ships. They eat together in a dining hall called the recruit galley. Recruits spend almost all of their time with groups. This helps them learn the importance of teamwork and working together.

Physical training includes daily running, swimming, push-ups, sit-ups, and chin-ups. U.S. Navy

Recruits stand in formation during boot camp. Boot camp teaches recruits how to think and act like a team.

personnel are warriors—they must be in good shape to fight. Physical training also includes drilling, such as marching in formation and standing at attention. Drilling is good teamwork training, because it forces people to think and act together as a unit.

In the classroom, recruits learn about the military. The second week of boot camp begins with classroom training. Courses focus on navy rules and how the navy works. Recruits learn about professionalism, the U.S. Navy chain of command (who takes orders from whom), and U.S. Navy customs and rules.

Recruits also learn about seamanship, or working at sea. They practice the many tasks involved in working on a ship. (Not every recruit will serve on a ship. But they all must learn these skills.)

At the end of boot camp, all recruits must pass a final test. The test includes battle stations, when a group of recruits is tested together on how well they handle battle situations. They perform practice drills, including fire drills, attack drills, and medical disaster drills. Recruits who pass battle stations and final written tests move on to advanced school. There they train in their ratings.

STANDING WATCHES

During navy boot camp, all recruits take turns standing watch, or guarding their "ships"—1,000-person barracks built to look like ships. Standing watch involves staying awake all night—often after grueling days of training—to make sure nobody comes in or out of the dormitory. And recruits who are unlucky enough to attend boot camp during winter must also take turns at "Snow Watch." This involves getting woken up to shovel snow in the middle of the night.

Recruits who want to join the Naval Special Warfare forces have to pass another physical test to go on to the next level. Those who want to join the SEALs must pass this physical test during boot camp. SEAL candidates have four chances to pass. Those who pass go on to advanced school as SEALs. Those who don't stay in the U.S. Navy and attend their chosen advanced school.

ADVANCED SCHOOL

At advanced school, or A School, navy recruits learn the skills they need to work on their source rates. During A School, recruits spend most of their time studying, taking classes, or receiving on-the-job training.

A School lasts from two weeks to two years, depending on the area. To graduate, recruits have to pass a series of tests in their specialties. Once they complete A School, recruits who are not going into the

A School students learn the basic and advanced skills to perform their specialized ratings.

Naval Special Warfare forces become enlisted sailors. They are sent to navy bases around the world to begin their naval careers.

Naval Special Warfare forces recruits go on to more training. SEAL candidates need to pass Basic Underwater Demolition/SEAL (BUD/S) training. Those who want to join SEAL delivery vehicle or special boat units take the Special Warfare Combatant Crewman (SWCC) course.

BASIC UNDERWATER DEMOLITION/SEAL (BUD/S) TRAINING

BUD/S training takes place at the Naval Special Warfare Center in Coronado, California. It is probably the toughest military training course in the world. BUD/S is the last

SEAL trainees never walk anywhere. They run to meals, to class, to training—even to the bathroom. The constant running gets them in excellent shape.

PUSH-UPS AS PUNISHMENT

SEAL trainees spend a lot of time doing push-ups. Nearly every training exercise starts and ends with them. When a trainee makes a mistake or can't complete an exercise, his entire team is ordered to do push-ups. When a team isn't moving fast enough, the instructor will order the team to "drop and give me twenty!" SEAL trainees probably do 1,000 or more push-ups every day.

When trainees become so strong that push-ups are too easy for them, instructors find other ways to challenge their men. One form of punishment involves making the team hold its inflatable boat over their heads for long periods of time. If this isn't hard enough, the instructor will make the team fill the boat with water to make it heavier. Such exercises are designed to make the SEALs as tough and strong as possible.

step for trainees who want to become SEALs. Officers and enlistees train together in this 27-week program. Only about 15 percent of candidates—less than one out of every five—will pass.

The first phase, or part, of BUD/S training gets the recruits in top shape. For eight weeks, they are pushed to their limits. They run, swim, and struggle through obstacle courses until they are ready to collapse. These exercises help instructors find out if the trainees have the strength and discipline to handle the toughest missions. Trainees say that BUD/S training makes regular navy boot camp seem easy.

Halfway through the first phase, the training gets even harder. That's when "Hell Week" begins. During this five-and-one-half-day test, recruits are allowed to sleep for a total of only four hours. They have to pass several physical tests, including timed ocean swims, a timed underwater swim, a timed run, and an obstacle course.

Hell Week ends with "So Sorry Day," when trainees have to pass through a brutal obstacle course. They will crawl through mud, swim through dirty and polluted water, and cross rope bridges. And trainees must do all of this through smoke and the sounds of

During Hell Week, recruits' physical, emotional, and mental strength are put to the ultimate test.

machine-gun fire and explosions all around them. More than one-third of SEAL trainees fail to pass Hell Week.

The second phase of the BUD/S course is combat diving training. This phase lasts for seven weeks. Trainees work in a swimming pool and in the ocean. They practice using scuba gear and learn how to fight underwater.

The third phase of BUD/S training is ground warfare. Trainees learn everything they need to know about weapons, fighting, and explosives during this 10-week phase. They become excellent sharpshooters, able to hit targets from long distances with a single shot. They also learn rappelling—the skill of dropping from a cliff or a helicopter by rope.

At the end of the ground warfare phase of BUD/S, trainees spend four weeks in a combat drill. They practice all the skills they have learned during training. Those who pass this drill become U.S. Navy SEALs, some of the best-trained fighters in the world.

But training doesn't end there. New SEALs report for parachute training right away. This is a three-week course, where they learn how to drop into enemy territory without being seen. And for SEALs, the training never stops. They are constantly practicing their skills.

TOOLS OF THE TRADE

NAVY SPECIAL FORCES depend on their minds and bodies to accomplish an operation. But they also rely on some of the best military equipment in the world to get the job done.

DEMOLITIONS
These explosive devices are used to blow up targets such as enemy bases, roads, or communication systems. They include dynamite sticks and C4 explosive, a claylike substance.

MP-5 SUBMACHINE GUN
The MP-5 *(right)* is a light gun that can rapidly fire many bullets. One reason SEALs use them is that they work well even after being in the water.

MARK V SPECIAL OPERATIONS CRAFT
The Mark V *(below)* are the newest and fastest boats used by navy special forces. These heavily armed boats can carry up to 16 SEALs and can travel more than 50 miles per hour.

Rigid-Hull Inflatable Boats (RIBs)

RIBs *(right)* are often used to transport SEALs to their missions. They are strong and light and can move quickly through shallow water. The bottom half of an RIB is made of fiberglass, a strong but light material that is made from tiny pieces of glass. The top half of an RIB is made from cloth.

Patrol Boats, Light (PBL)

PBLs are used by SBUs to observe waterways such as rivers and beaches. They are 25 feet long and can go up to 40 miles per hour. They are armed with two light machine guns.

SEAL Delivery Vehicles (SDVs)

SDVs are "wet" submarines—the occupants get wet when they go underwater. SEALs use these types of vehicles to travel secretly underwater.

Advanced SEAL Delivery System

These vehicles are "dry" submarines, used to deliver SEALs to an insertion or infiltration point.

Global Positioning Systems (GPS)

GPS *(right)* are small, handheld computers that use radio signals to help SEALs locate places and objects.

SPECIAL WARFARE COMBATANT CREWMAN (SWCC) TRAINING

The SWCC course trains men for the special boat units (SBU) and SEAL delivery vehicle (SDV) units. This class also takes place in Coronado, California. Although not as tough as BUD/S training, the course is very difficult. About one-quarter of the recruits who begin SWCC do not finish.

SWCC training lasts for nine weeks and combines physical conditioning with military instruction. During the first part of the course, recruits learn about the different kinds of boats used in SBU and SDV units. Members of these units must know how to perform all of the duties on each boat. That way, if a crewmember is injured or killed during a mission, anyone can take his place and finish the job.

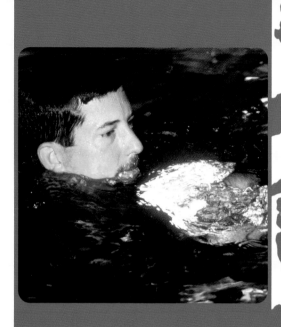

DROWNPROOFING

Every SEAL trainee goes through drownproofing. During these exercises, each man is tossed in a deep pool with his legs tied together and his arms tied behind his back. Trainees learn how to swim up to the surface, take a breath of air *(above)*, and then float back underwater. In time, they will be able to spend hours in the water like this without drowning. They also learn how to free their tied-up hands and feet while underwater.

During SWCC, recruits also work on their physical conditioning. They do daily push-ups, sit-ups, and runs. They have to learn to swim fast while wearing their uniforms.

SWCC recruits spend their last two weeks of training on San Clement Island, off the coast of California. Here the recruits learn about weapons. They also learn how to fight and to hide from the enemy if their boats are destroyed. When recruits finish this exercise, they become SBU or SDV unit members. They are ready to perform special operations anywhere they are needed around the world.

SWCC members perform a practice mission on a narrow river beach under hostile fire conditions.

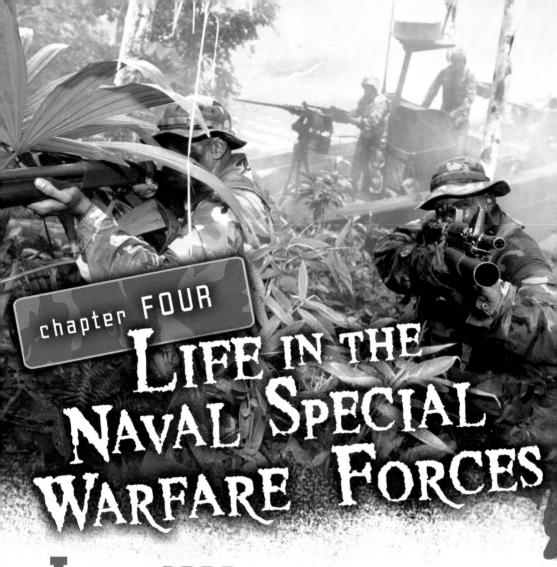

chapter FOUR

LIFE IN THE NAVAL SPECIAL WARFARE FORCES

IN THE 2000S, the U.S. Naval Special
Warfare forces have about 5,000 members. They
perform missions in all parts of the world. For these
people, life is rarely dull. They are constantly
challenged in many different ways. Naval Special
Warfare forces units must be ready to report for a
mission anywhere in the world within 72 hours.

Usually, SEAL, SBU, and SDV units work together to
carry out missions. Often these missions are clandestine,
or secret. The U.S. government does not tell the public

many details of these missions. Military leaders do not want enemies to know what special forces members can do. They also do not want the enemy to know how or where the special forces perform their missions.

Preparation and teamwork are the two keys to the success of Naval Special Warfare forces. Most missions are carefully planned. Naval Special Warfare forces units are always prepared for whatever might happen during a job. This is why their training is so extreme and why they continue to train throughout their naval careers. Teamwork is also essential. Naval Special Warfare forces members have to be able to count on every member of their team. More often than not, their survival and the success of the mission depend upon everyone doing the job correctly.

Details are kept secret from the general public. But some basic facts are known about Naval Special Warfare forces missions. They usually fall into one of three kinds of jobs— combat and rescue missions, humanitarian missions, and training.

WARNING ORDERS

Before each mission, every member of a navy special forces team receives a warning order. This is a paper that describes the upcoming operation. The warning order lists what supplies will be necessary for the mission. The order also says how long the operation will last. Team members need this information to prepare for the job.

Many missions are clandestine. In these cases, the warning order may include very little information. Sometimes team members do not even know what part of the world they are going to. Thanks to their training, however, Naval Special Warfare forces team members can still be prepared for just about anything that comes up in an operation.

INSIGNIA

LIKE ALL OF THE U.S. ARMED FORCES, the U.S. Navy is organized according to rank. A person of lower rank is required to follow the orders of a person of higher rank. For example, a seaman recruit, the lowest rank in the navy, must follow the orders of a petty officer or an ensign. The highest naval rank is four-star admiral. Here are some insignia, starting with the lowest rank and moving up to the highest.

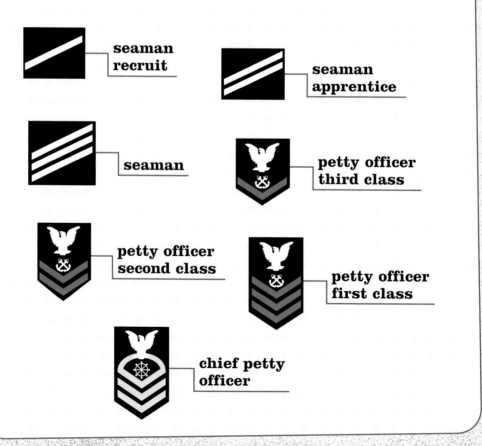

seaman recruit

seaman apprentice

seaman

petty officer third class

petty officer second class

petty officer first class

chief petty officer

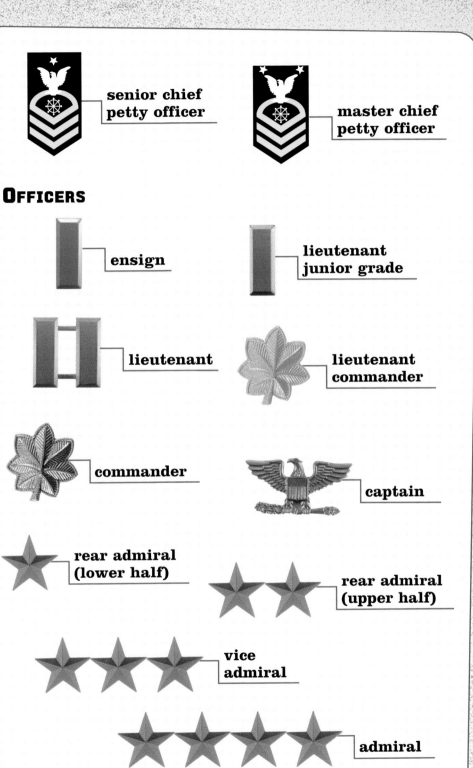

senior chief
petty officer

master chief
petty officer

Officers

ensign

lieutenant
junior grade

lieutenant

lieutenant
commander

commander

captain

rear admiral
(lower half)

rear admiral
(upper half)

vice
admiral

admiral

COMBAT AND RESCUE MISSIONS

U.S. Naval Special Warfare forces perform many
different kinds of combat missions. Not all of these
operations involve attacking or killing the enemy.
SEALs are often called on to perform reconnaissance,
or recon, missions. During recon missions, SEAL
teams infiltrate enemy territory to find out certain
information. Usually, this information will be used to
plan an attack. For example, a team may be sent into
enemy territory to find the exact location of an enemy
base or an enemy building. Depending on the situation,
SBU, SDV units, or helicopters insert the SEAL team in
the general area of the target. The SEALs then make
their way to the spot on their own.

During a recon mission, SEALs might use special laptop computers
to send back pictures of enemy territory to their units.

Often the SEALs are not called on to attack the location. Attacking is usually too risky, especially if the enemy has hundreds of well-armed soldiers in the area. Instead, the SEALs draw detailed maps of the area. They mark target areas on the map. Then they sneak back out of the area without being seen. Later, the military may call in aircraft to bomb the target or send in a large force of soldiers and vehicles to attack.

The military often uses search-and-rescue missions to rescue U.S. personnel who have been shot down or

Sometimes the best way to get behind enemy lines is by parachute jump.

captured by the enemy. For these missions, SEALs may be inserted behind enemy lines. Insertion is usually done by helicopter or parachute jump or with the help of a SDV or SBU unit. Sometimes search-and-rescue missions take civilians (people who aren't in the military) out of dangerous situations. Search-and-rescue missions can be dangerous because SEALs often have to attack well-armed locations where they are outnumbered. They may have to kill enemies while trying not to kill friendly combatants.

Another common special operation is the precision strike mission. During these operations, special forces units attack an enemy target, such as a bridge, a communication center, a terrorist base, or a military base. They might also be called on to capture or kill important people, such as terrorist leaders or wanted criminals.

When time allows, SEAL teams often practice and train for specific missions. Every team member will learn his role and where he will need to be before and after the shooting starts. Once inserted, SEAL teams will make it to their targets quickly and quietly. SEAL attacks are swift and powerful. They often last just a few minutes. During the wars in Afghanistan and Iraq, SEAL teams targeted and destroyed

U.S. Navy Special Warfare forces continue to locate and destroy ammunition *(above)* seized during missions in Iraq.

terrorist hideouts. They blew up bridges and military bases and captured important prisoners.

HUMANITARIAN AND LAW ENFORCEMENT MISSIONS

In the past, U.S. Naval Special Warfare forces have been called on to help in humanitarian missions. For instance, the United States has helped deliver food and medicine to people in Somalia and in Bosnia, an Eastern European country that was torn apart by war in the 1990s.

Naval Special Warfare forces also help rescue people from natural disasters such as floods and hurricanes. During floods, SBUs might be called into action. SBU boats can move around in very shallow water and rescue people stranded in floods.

SBUs also help the U.S. government to fight the trafficking (transporting) of illegal drugs. When the government suspects that a boat or ship is carrying illegal drugs, an SBU may be called in to capture the boat. Drug traffickers often carry guns and other weapons, so SBUs must be ready to fight if necessary.

WORKING TOGETHER

All branches of the U.S. military have special operations forces. For instance, the U.S. Army has Airborne Rangers. These teams are often sent to scout out battle sites before the regular army troops arrive. The air force has several units of pararescue troops. These highly trained units are dropped behind enemy lines to rescue pilots who have been shot down inside enemy territory. SEAL, SBU, and SDV members generally train together and are sent together to missions around the world. Sometimes they work with other U.S. special operations forces, such as Army Airborne Rangers and the air force's pararescue teams.

TRAINING

When not on a mission, special forces teams are usually training. SEALs spend much of their time running and swimming to stay in top physical shape. SEALs also train with weapons, explosives, scuba equipment, and vehicles.

A big part of training involves practice missions. SEAL teams, SDV teams, and SBUs are constantly

These EOD divers are working with an underwater mine during training exercises in Guantánamo Bay, Cuba.

planning and carrying out practice missions. These exercises keep members in top shape and ready for action. Often Naval Special Warfare forces units perform training missions with other branches of the U.S. armed forces, including the army, air force, Marine Corps, and Coast Guard.

In addition to training for themselves, navy special forces units help train soldiers and sailors from other countries. They teach the skills that they have learned during their own training, including how to perform clandestine missions. SBU and SDV units teach sailors how to operate small boats in shallow water. Naval Special Warfare forces have trained soldiers and sailors in Asia, Central America, Europe, and the Middle East.

SEALs take training very seriously. On a dangerous mission, good preparation can save lives. The SEALs have a saying: "The more you sweat in peacetime, the less you will bleed in war."

THE FUTURE: FIGHTING TERRORISM AROUND THE WORLD

After the September 11, 2001, attacks on the United States, fighting terrorism has become more important than ever for the U.S. armed forces. Special forces are playing a key role in hunting down terrorists. U.S. Naval Special Warfare forces are working hard to find and destroy terrorists before they can attack the United States. To help with the fight, the U.S. Navy is training more and more SEALs and SBUs.

SEAL teams are at work in Iraq and Afghanistan. They are training soldiers for new armed forces in these countries. And they are hunting down fighters who are attacking the new governments of Iraq and Afghanistan. SEAL teams are also working with soldiers from other countries to fight terrorism. These kinds of missions, where soldiers from different countries work on the same team, are called joint operations.

More than one-half of the world's population lives within one mile of an ocean or large river. This means that the amphibious skills of Naval Special Warfare forces are constantly needed. They are ready to defend the United States and its allies and to wipe out terrorists. And they will continue to perform humanitarian missions to help people in need around the world.

Preparation and teamwork continue to be the two main keys to the success of the Naval Special Warfare forces. Through constant practice and training, they are always ready to get the job done wherever they are needed around the world.

THE HUNT FOR BIN LADEN

Deep in the mountainous caves of a remote part of Afghanistan *(above)*, a top Navy SEAL commander leads a secretive strike force named Task Force 121. Task Force 121 has one mission: to find Osama bin Laden and cripple the terrorist network al-Qaeda. Al-Qaeda is suspected of carrying out the September 11, 2001, terrorist attacks in New York City and Washington, D.C. Bin Laden is believed to be hiding out among the rocky caves in Afghanistan. Task Force 121—a combination of U.S. special forces units including Navy SEALs and Army Delta Force troops, as well as top Central Intelligence Agency (CIA) agents—is the best hope for capturing the terrorist leader.

Leading this elite group of spies and fighters is a top Navy SEAL commander named Bill McRaven. McRaven first served as a Navy SEAL in combat in Vietnam. After the September 11 attacks, he helped draft the U.S. government's plan to fight terrorism. In 2003 he took control of Task Force 121 and helped capture Saddam Hussein in Iraq. Then Task Force 121 turned its attention to bin Laden.

McRaven and his troops receive briefs (reports) from CIA agents every day. They have the latest technology, including a computer software program called Analyst Notebook. Analyst Notebook uses information to pin down the exact whereabouts of criminals and other elusive figures.

STRUCTURE

THE PRESIDENT OF THE UNITED STATES is the commander in chief of all U.S. armed forces. The secretary of defense is in charge of all of the armed forces and reports directly to the president. A civilian, the secretary of the navy, is in charge of the navy. The navy's highest-ranking military post is chief of naval operations (CNO). The CNO is a four star admiral.

The Naval Special Warfare Command in Coronado, California, is in charge of all Naval Special Warfare units. The command is divided into four naval special warfare groups (NSWG-1, NSWG-2, NSWG-3, NSWG-4) and the Naval Special Warfare Center (NSWC). The NSWC is in charge of training new special forces operatives. NSWG-1 and NSWG-2 each have four SEAL teams, while NSWG-3 and NSWG-4 are in charge of the navy's SBU and SDV teams. The groups are headquartered on two naval bases—one in Coronado and one in Norfolk, Virginia.

PRESIDENT OF THE UNITED STATES

SECRETARY OF DEFENSE

SECRETARY OF THE NAVY

CHIEF OF NAVAL OPERATIONS

NAVAL SPECIAL WARFARE COMMAND

NSWG-1
NSWG-2
SEALS

NSWG-3
NSWG-4
SBUS
SDVS

NSWC

TIMELINE

1775   The Continental Navy is formed to fight against the British in the American Revolution (1775–1783).

1794   The U.S. Congress forms the U.S. Navy.

1941   The United States enters World War II. The U.S. Navy organizes special units, including navy combat demolition units (NCDUs) and underwater demolition teams (UDTs). Patrol torpedo (PT) boats are used for the first time.

1944   NCDUs clear the beaches for Operation Overlord, the June 6 Allied landing at Normandy, France.

1950–1953   Navy special forces perform dangerous missions during the Korean War.

1962   The first SEAL and UDT units are sent to Vietnam.

1966   Patrol boats, riverine (PBR) see action for the first time in Vietnam.

1983   Naval Special Warfare forces invade the Caribbean island of Grenada during Operation Urgent Fury.

1989   Naval Special Warfare forces invade Panama to help capture General Manuel Noriega during Operation Just Cause.

1990   Naval Special Warfare forces are sent to the Middle East in response to the Iraqi invasion of Kuwait.

1991   Naval Special Warfare forces play a key role in the Persian Gulf War against Iraq.

1992–1994   Naval Special Warfare forces help in the delivery of humanitarian aid during Operation Restore Hope in Somalia.

2001–2002   Naval Special Warfare forces help fight the Taliban and al-Qaeda in Afghanistan.

2003–present   Naval Special Warfare forces serve in Operation Iraq Freedom in Iraq.

GLOSSARY

amphibious: taking place on land, sea, and sometimes through the air

Basic Underwater Demolition/SEAL (BUD/S) training: an extreme training course that navy enlistees and officers must pass to become SEALs

boot camp: a common term for basic military training. Boot camp is the first training for enlisted members of the army, navy, air force, and the Marine Corps.

civilian: a person who does not belong to a military organization

clandestine: secret. Naval Special Warfare forces often perform clandestine missions.

combat: fighting

demolition: destroying something with explosives

infiltrate: to pass through enemy lines

mission: a task performed by a military unit

rebels: people who try to take over a country's government

Special Warfare Combatant Crewman (SWCC) training: a nine-week training course for navy enlistees or officers who want to join an SBU or SDV unit

terrorists: people who use violence—often against civilians—to achieve their goals

warning orders: papers given to Naval Special Warfare forces members describing the tasks of an upcoming mission

FAMOUS PEOPLE

Command Master Chief Rudy Boesch (born 1928) Born in Virginia Beach, Virginia, Boesch served during World War II as a member of a Scout and Raider unit. In 1951 he joined the navy's UDT, and in 1962, he became a SEAL. He served in the Naval Special Warfare forces for more than 45 years. Boesch won fame in 2000, when he appeared on the popular TV series "Survivor."

Lieutenant Joseph (Bob) Kerrey (born 1943) Born in Lincoln, Nebraska, Kerrey served as a SEAL in Vietnam in the 1960s. He lost part of his right leg during one of his missions there. He was awarded the United States' highest decoration, the Congressional Medal of Honor for his bravery. He went on to serve Nebraska in the U. S. Senate from 1988 to 2000.

Lieutenant Thomas R. Norris (born 1944) Born in Jacksonville, Florida, Norris served as a Navy SEAL in the Vietnam War. He completed two daring missions to rescue two wounded U.S. airmen who had been shot down deep inside enemy territory. A year later, Norris received a near-fatal head wound in battle. Norris's injuries ended his SEAL career. But he went on to work in the U.S. Federal Bureau of Investigation for more than 20 years.

Petty Officer Michael E. Thornton (born 1949) Thornton was born in Greenville, South Carolina. He served as a Navy SEAL in the Vietnam War, earning the Congressional Medal of Honor for the courageous rescue of Lieutenant Thomas R. Norris. On October 31, 1972, Thornton, Norris, and others set out on a reconnaissance mission inside enemy territory. The team soon came under fire, and Norris was wounded in the head. After slinging Norris over his shoulder, Thornton sprinted through a hail of enemy bullets to get both of them to safety.

Petty Officer Third Class Jesse Ventura (born 1951) Born James George Janos in Minneapolis, Minnesota, Ventura joined the U.S. Navy after high school and served with UDT 12 from 1969 to 1973. Since then he has been a professional wrestler, actor, radio talk show host, and mayor of a Minneapolis suburb. Ventura became the 38th governor of Minnesota in 1998 as part of the Reform Party, serving one term. In spring 2004, he became a visiting fellow at the Institute of Politics at Harvard's John F. Kennedy School of Government.

BIBLIOGRAPHY

Boehm, Roy, and Charles W. Sasser. *First SEAL.* New York: Simon & Schuster, 1997.

———. *U.S. Navy Special Forces: SEAL Teams.* Mankato, MN: Capstone Books, 2000.

———. *U.S. Navy Special Forces: Special Boat Units.* Mankato, MN: Capstone Books, 2000.

Chalker, Dennis. *One Perfect OP: An Insider's Account of the Navy SEAL Special Warfare Teams.* New York: William Morrow, 2002.

Dockery, Kevin. *Navy SEALs: A History of the Early Years.* New York: Berkley Books, 2001.

Halberstadt, Hans. *U.S. Navy SEALs in Action.* Osceola, WI: Motorbooks International, 1995.

Hollenbeck, Cliff, and Dick Couch. *To Be a U.S. Navy SEAL.* St. Paul, MN: MBI Publishing Company, 2003.

Naval Historical Center: A History of the U.S. Navy
http://www.history.navy.mil/history/history1.htm
Visit this site to learn more about the history of the U.S. Navy, including the navy's special forces units.

Naval Special Warfare Command: Missions and History
https://www.navsoc.navy.mil/history.htm
This official U.S. Navy website offers articles and related information on the history and missions of the U.S. Navy Special Warfare Command.

SpecWarNet: U.S. Navy SEALs
http://www.specwarnet.com/americas/SEALs.htm
This unofficial website of U.S. special forces provides a history and description of the U.S. Navy SEALs.

FURTHER READING

Cornish, Geoff. *Battlefield Support.* Minneapolis: Lerner Publications Company, 2003.

———. *Tanks.* Minneapolis: Lerner Publications Company, 2003.

Dartford, Mark. *Helicopters.* Minneapolis: Lerner Publications Company, 2003.

———. *Warships.* Minneapolis: Lerner Publications Company, 2003.

Doyle, Kevin. *Submarines.* Minneapolis: Lerner Publications Company, 2003.

Kennedy, Robert C. *Life with the Navy SEALS*. New York: Children's Press, 2000.

Streissguth, Tom. *U.S. Navy SEALs: Serving Your Country*. Mankato, MN: Capstone Press, 1996.

WEBSITES

Naval Special Warfare
http://www.sealchallenge.navy.mil/
This website, developed by the Naval Special Warfare Command, has information about different Naval Special Warfare forces units, including SEALs and SWCC.

Naval Special Warfare Command
https://www.navsoc.navy.mil/
This website features news and information about the Naval Special Warfare forces.

Navy.com
http://www.navy.com/
Visit the U.S. Navy's official website for recruiting information and the latest U.S. Navy news.

Navy.com: Explore the Navy: U.S. Navy SEALs
http://www.navy.com/seals
Learn more about the U.S. Navy SEALs, including the SEAL training program and the high-tech equipment they use, at this site.

Official U.S. Navy SEAL Information Website
https://www.seal.navy.mil/seal/bec_intro.asp
Find out how to become a Navy SEAL at the navy's official SEAL website.

U.S. Naval Academy
http://www.usna.edu
The U.S. Naval Academy's website has news and information from the academy, as well as information about how to become a midshipman.

INDEX

ABOUT THE AUTHOR

Sandy Donovan has written numerous books for young readers on topics including history, civics, and biology. Donovan has also worked as a newspaper reporter and a magazine editor. She holds a bachelor's degree in journalism and a master's degree in public policy. Her titles include *The U.S. Air Force, The Channel Tunnel, Making Laws: A Look at How a Bill Becomes a Law, Protecting America: A Look at the People Who Keep Our Country Safe,* and *Running for Office: A Look at Political Campaigns.* Donovan lives in Minneapolis, Minnesota, with her husband and two sons.

PHOTO ACKNOWLEDGMENTS

The images in this book are used with the permission of: © U.S. Naval Photos provided by Navy Visual News Service, Washington, D.C., pp. 4, 6, 7, 17, 18, 20, 21, 22, 23, 24, 25, 26, 28 (both), 30, 31, 32, 35, 38 (top), 40 (bottom), 41 (top), 43, 48, 49, 50, 52, 53, 55; © Naval Academy Museum, p. 5; © Hulton-Deutsch Collection/CORBIS, p. 8; © Hulton|Archive by Getty Images, p. 10; © John F. Kennedy Library, p. 11; Photograph VA000117, December 1967, John Brady Collection, The Vietnam Archive, Texas Tech University, p. 12; © Tim Page/CORBIS, p. 13; © Defense Visual Information Center, pp. 15, 16, 19, 33, 42; © Dave Bartruff/ CORBIS, p. 27; © Robert Bruce Military Photo Features, p. 29 (right); © Lynsey Addario/CORBIS, p. 29 (left); © James A. Sugar/CORBIS, pp. 36, 41 (bottom); © CORBIS, p. 38 (bottom); © Heckler and Koch Defense, p. 40 (top); © Leif Skoogfors/CORBIS, p. 44; © Erin Liddell/Independent Picture Service, pp. 46, 47 (top two); © Todd Strand/ Independent Picture Service, p. 47 (bottom 10).

Cover: Defense Visual Information Center.